M000280507

CARPE DIEM

DIEM

summersdale

CARPE DIEM

This edition copyright © Summersdale Publishers Ltd, 2022
First published in 2013
Reprinted as *Seize the Day* in 2016 and as *Carpe Diem* in 2017

An Hachette UK Company
www.hachette.co.uk

Summersdale Publishers Ltd
Part of Octopus Publishing Group Limited
Carmelite House
50 Victoria Embankment
LONDON
EC4Y 0DZ
UK

www.summersdale.com

Printed and bound in China

ISBN: 978-1-80007-186-5

Substantial discounts on bulk quantities of Summersdale books are available to corporations, professional associations and other organizations. For details contact general enquiries: telephone: +44 (0) 1243 771107 or email: enquiries@summersdale.com.

To..

From......................................

The envious moment is flying now, now, while we're speaking: seize the day.

Horace

When's the best time to start? Right now!

With the new day
comes new strength
and new thoughts.

Eleanor Roosevelt

YOU DO CREATE YOUR OWN DESTINY.

Daniel Radcliffe

BE A CHILD AGAIN TODAY, AND SPREAD SOME MISCHIEF!

You are never too old to set another goal or to dream a new dream.

Les Brown

**Act as if what
you do makes a
difference. It does.**

William James

Build
something
new today,
however
small

Opportunities multiply as they are seized.

Sun Tzu

I'd rather regret
the things I've
done than regret
the things I
haven't done.

Lucille Ball

Without obstacles, life would just be a race – and that wouldn't be half as much fun

**If you're going
through hell,
keep going.**

Winston Churchill

In the middle of
difficulty lies
opportunity.

Albert Einstein

SHARE THE FUN WHEREVER YOU GO TODAY

One may walk over the highest mountain one step at a time.

John Wanamaker

Wherever you are
– be all there.

Jim Elliot

BE A GIFT TO THE WORLD TODAY

Things do not happen. Things are made to happen.

John F. Kennedy

We are all in the gutter but some of us are looking at the stars.

Oscar Wilde

Good things come to those who... go out and get them!

If you ask me what
I came into this
life to do, I will
tell you: I came to
live out loud.

Émile Zola

WHO
SEEKS
SHALL
FIND.

Sophocles

EVERY
CHANGE
BRINGS
OPPORTUNITY
WITH IT

Whenever you fall, pick something up.

Oswald Avery

Tell me, what is it you plan to do with your one wild and precious life?

Mary Oliver

Who cares about winning or losing? Life is about taking part

Either you run the day or the day runs you.

Jim Rohn

Expect problems
and eat them for
breakfast.

Alfred A. Montapert

Make it happen!

The most effective way to do it, is to do it.

Amelia Earhart

Turn your face
to the sun and
the shadows fall
behind you.

Māori proverb

LISTEN TO YOUR INNER VOICE

**To know oneself,
one should
assert oneself.**

Albert Camus

You must be the change you wish to see in the world.

Mahatma Gandhi

YOU ARE THE
HERO OF
YOUR STORY

In order to
succeed, we must
first believe
that we can.

Nikos Kazantzakis

Nothing really matters except what you do now in this instant of time.

Eileen Caddy

What are you waiting for?

I have never met
a man so ignorant
that I couldn't
learn something
from him.

Galileo Galilei

I CAN, THEREFORE I AM.

Simone Weil

MAKE A
WISH... THEN
MAKE IT
COME TRUE!

No one knows what he can do till he tries.

Publilius Syrus

Life is a shipwreck, but we must not forget to sing in the lifeboats.

Voltaire

Who's that in the mirror? Looks like a go-getter to me

Whether you think you can or you think you can't, you're right.

Henry Ford

Life isn't about
finding yourself.
Life is about
creating yourself.

George Bernard Shaw

When life throws tomatoes at you, make a Bloody Mary

With the past, I have nothing to do; nor with the future. I live now.

Ralph Waldo Emerson

When you reach the
end of your rope,
tie a knot in it
and hang on.

Anonymous

YOU ONLY
LIVE ONCE

Perseverance is failing nineteen times and succeeding the twentieth.

Julie Andrews

Opportunity does not knock – it presents itself when you beat down the door.

Kyle Chandler

SQUEEZE ALL
THE JUICE
OUT OF
TODAY

Begin to be now
what you will
be hereafter.

William James

Set your goals high, and don't stop till you get there.

Bo Jackson

Your life is a work of art – it deserves to be seen

Nothing is a waste of
time if you use the
experience wisely.

Auguste Rodin

IT'S ALWAYS TOO EARLY TO QUIT.

Norman Vincent Peale

DON'T RACE FOR THE FINISH LINE: ENJOY THE JOURNEY

Find ecstasy in life; the mere sense of living is joy enough.

Emily Dickinson

If you wait, all that happens is that you get older.

Mario Andretti

Make every
minute count

One joy scatters a hundred griefs.

Chinese proverb

How wonderful it is
that nobody need
wait a single moment
before starting to
improve the world.

Anne Frank

Grab a double helping of life, with a side order of adventure

It's OK to have butterflies in your stomach. Just get them to fly in formation.

Rob Gilbert

Life is either a
daring adventure
or nothing.

Helen Keller

LIFE IS SWEET: TAKE A BIG BITE!

Opportunities are like sunrises. If you wait too long, you miss them.

William Arthur Ward

There are always flowers for those who want to see them.

Henri Matisse

TO REST IS TO RUST: STAY SHINY AND BRIGHT!

You're the
blacksmith of your
own happiness.

Swedish proverb

For myself, I am an optimist – it does not seem to be much use being anything else.

Winston Churchill

Every dawn is a new beginning, a time to start a new story

Live your questions now, and perhaps even without knowing it, you will live along some distant day into your answers.

Rainer Maria Rilke

THE SECRET OF GETTING AHEAD IS GETTING STARTED.

Anonymous

SING A
SONG, PAINT
A PICTURE...
CHANGE THE
WORLD

Some days there won't be a song in your heart. Sing anyway.

Emory Austin

You are perfectly
cast in your life.
I can't imagine
anyone but you in
the role. Go play.

Lin-Manuel Miranda

Why watch
TV when real
life is so much
more exciting?

The wise does at once what the fool does at last.

Baltasar Gracián

You can't use
up creativity. The
more you use, the
more you have.

Maya Angelou

Keep calm and seize the day

Live today for tomorrow it will all be history.

Proverb

Be happy. It's one
way of being wise.

Colette

LIVE YOUR
DREAMS

If you can find a path with no obstacles, it probably doesn't lead anywhere.

Frank A. Clark

There are no shortcuts to any place worth going.

Beverly Sills

LIVE LIFE OFF THE MAP AND BE YOUR OWN COMPASS

A journey of a
thousand miles
begins with a
single step.

Lao Tzu

Do not pray for an easy life. Pray for the strength to endure a difficult one.

Bruce Lee

Talk to someone new. You could make their day – and they might make yours

Life is simple,
it's just not easy.

Anonymous

EVERY ARTIST WAS FIRST AN AMATEUR.

Ralph Waldo Emerson

YOU ARE
A SONG:
MAKE SURE
YOU'RE
HEARD

To me, every hour of the day and night is an unspeakably perfect miracle.

Walt Whitman

Life shrinks or expands according to one's courage.

Anaïs Nin

Look at
life from
unexpected
angles today

The best way to make your dreams come true is to wake up.

Paul Valéry

To succeed in life,
you need three
things: a wishbone,
a backbone and a
funny bone.

Reba McEntire

Be who
you've always
wanted to be

Life is a helluva lot more fun if you say "yes" rather than "no".

Richard Branson

Look at life through the windshield, not the rear-view mirror.

Byrd Baggett

MAKE
YOUR OWN
SUNSHINE

**The best way out
is always through.**

Robert Frost

**Look at everything
as though you were
seeing it for the
first or last time.**

Betty Smith

YOU CAN DO IT: ALL YOU HAVE TO DO IS TRY

The man who removes
a mountain begins
by carrying away
small stones.

Chinese proverb

Scared is what you're feeling... brave is what you're doing.

Emma Donoghue

Just be
yourself

If your ship
doesn't come in,
swim out to it.

Jonathan Winters

LIFE BEGINS AT THE END OF YOUR COMFORT ZONE.

Neale Donald Walsch

LIFE IS NOT A REHEARSAL: ENJOY THE LIMELIGHT!

Do your thing and don't care if they like it.

Tina Fey

What matters is to live in the present, live now, for every moment is now.

Sathya Sai Baba

Enjoy today and don't worry about tomorrow

I have found that if you love life, life will love you back.

Arthur Rubinstein

If you're already
walking on thin
ice, you might as
well dance.

Proverb

Go and get it!

It's important not to limit yourself. You can do whatever you really love to do, no matter what it is.

Ryan Gosling

Don't get your knickers in a knot. Nothing is solved and it just makes you walk funny.

Kathryn Carpenter

NOBODY CAN HOLD YOU BACK

You can have
anything you want
if you will give up
the belief that you
can't have it.

Robert Anthony

You can't expect to hit the jackpot if you don't put a few nickels in the machine.

Flip Wilson

SHOW THE WORLD WHAT YOU'RE MADE OF

Change your life
today. Don't gamble
on the future, act
now, without delay.

Simone de Beauvoir

Life isn't about waiting for the storm to pass; it's about learning to dance in the rain.

Anonymous

Dress to impress and be the best you can be

Shoot for the moon.
Even if you miss,
you'll land among
the stars.

Les Brown

IF THE WIND WILL NOT SERVE, TAKE TO THE OARS.

Latin proverb

YOU'RE
NEVER LOST:
YOU'RE JUST
DISCOVERING
NEW PLACES

Happiness is a way of travel, not a destination.

Roy M. Goodman

Opportunity is missed by most people because it is dressed in overalls and looks like work.

Thomas Edison

Turn your
hopes into
realities

Difficulties strengthen the mind, as labour does the body.

Seneca the Younger

Our greatest glory is not in never falling, but in rising every time we fall.

Confucius

Make an impression!

First say to yourself what you would be; and then do what you have to do.

Epictetus

Luck is a dividend
of sweat. The more
you sweat, the
luckier you get.

Ray Kroc

WELCOME
TODAY'S
CHALLENGES

You can't wait for inspiration. You have to go after it with a club.

Jack London

When you come to a roadblock, take a detour.

Mary Kay Ash

SPOT THE
FLOWERS
THAT GROW
UP THROUGH
THE CRACKS

The season of
failure is the best
time for sowing the
seeds of success.

Paramahansa Yogananda

It's never too late
– never too late to
start over, never too
late to be happy.

Jane Fonda

Today is a blank page – what are you going to write on it?

You can't turn
back the clock but
you can wind it
up again.

Bonnie Prudden

WHOEVER IS HAPPY WILL MAKE OTHERS HAPPY TOO.

Anne Frank

MAKE NEW
CONNECTIONS
TODAY!

I couldn't wait for success, so I went ahead without it.

Jonathan Winters

**Nothing will work
unless you do.**

Maya Angelou

Doors are
made to be
opened; locks
are made to
fit a key

When it is darkest, men see the stars.

Ralph Waldo Emerson

A mind is like
a parachute. It
doesn't work if it
is not open.

Frank Zappa

Do what you can, with what you have, where you are.

Theodore Roosevelt

**CARPE
DIEM**

Have you enjoyed this book?
If so, find us on Facebook at
Summersdale Publishers, on Twitter
at @Summersdale and on Instagram
at @summersdalebooks and get in
touch. We'd love to hear from you!

www.summersdale.com